LINA'S BIG DEPARTURE

Today is a big day for Lina. She has finally arrived at the city's karting track. The engines roar, and the smell of gasoline fills the air. Lina smiles, her eyes shining with excitement.

"I'm going to become a karting driver!" she says, looking at her friend Jules.
Jules, always ready for adventure, replies, "Let's go, Lina! The race is waiting for us!"

ESSENTIAL EQUIPMENT

"To be a good driver, you need good equipment!" Lina explains. "Look, here's my helmet!" She shows off her colorful helmet. "It protects my head. And my suit is special for karting!"

Jules watches her while wearing his own gear. "And let's not forget the gloves and shoes!" he adds. "All of this keeps us safe during the race!"

DISCOVERY OF KARTING

Lina and Jules walk over to a shiny kart.
"It has wheels that spin fast, a steering wheel to guide it, and pedals to accelerate and brake," Jules points to the engine. "And this is the engine! It's what makes the kart go."
Lina nods in agreement. "Yes, every part is important for the race!"

Exhaust

Engine

Pedal

Steering Wheel

Seat

Nassau Panel

Bumper

Wheel

Ponton

SAFETY FIRST

Before getting into the karts, Lina and Jules listen to the instructor. "Safety is paramount!" the instructor says. "You must always wear your helmet and follow the rules." Lina smiles and says to Jules, "That's true, it's better to be cautious to have fun!"

RED
Important danger, I stop.

YELLOW
Moderate danger, I slow down.

BLUE
When overtaking, I let the driver behind me pass.

CHECKERED
End of the race, deceleration and return to the pits.

FRENCH FLAG
Race start.

RED CROSS
Emergency intervention, slow down immediately.

BLACK
The driver must immediately return to the driver park.

BLACK AND WHITE
Warning about dangerous driving.

BLACK AND RED
Stop for technical issues; the driver must stop.

RED YELLOW
Tire change.

THE START OF THE RACE

The long-awaited moment has finally arrived. Lina and Jules stand behind the starting line, their karts ready to go.
"I'm so excited!" Lina exclaimed. Jules nudges her.
"Ready to go?" he asks.
"Ready!" Lina replies with a big smile. The engines roar, and the starting signal is given. "Let's race!"

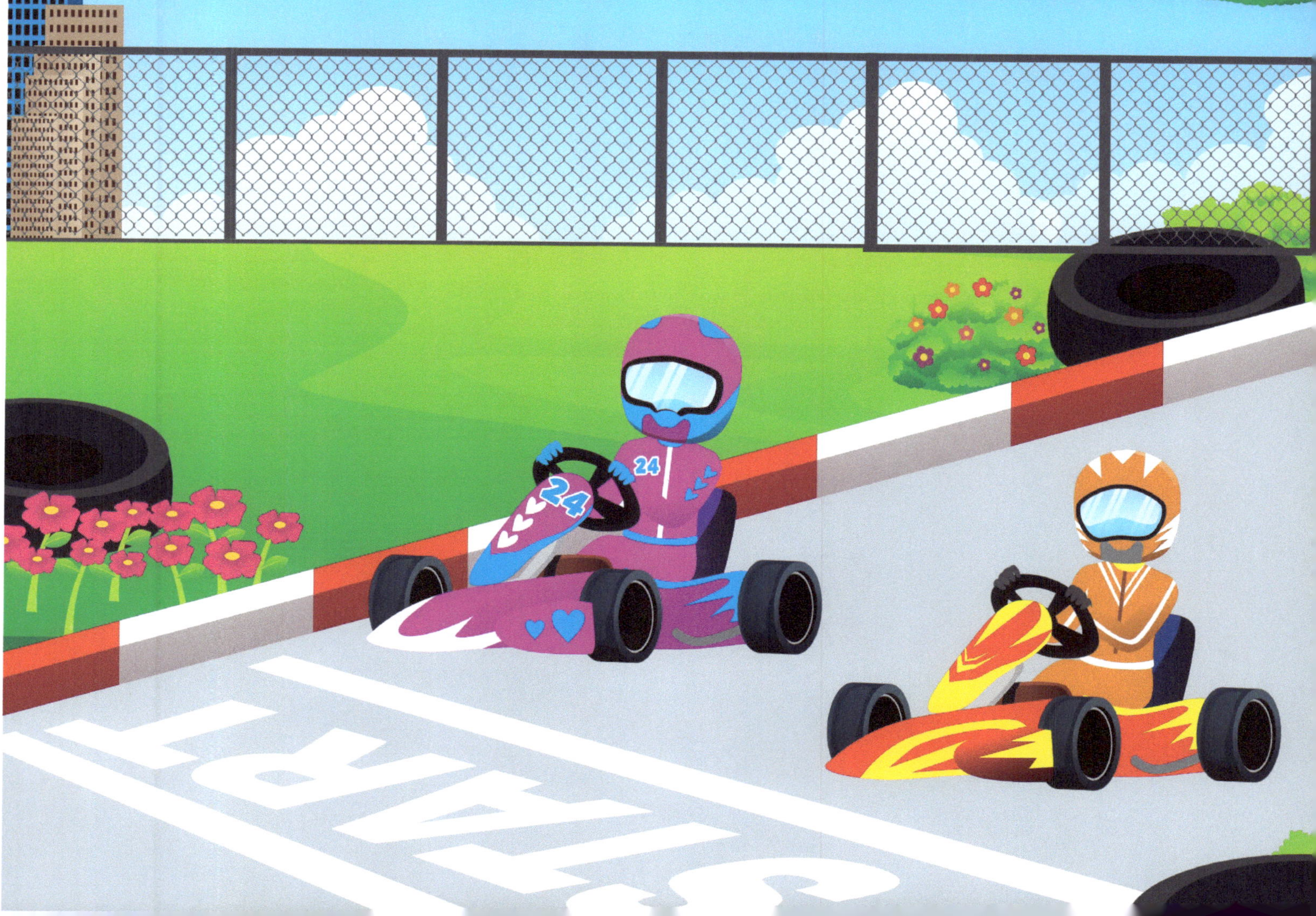

THE INTENSITY OF THE RACE

The karts zoom around the track. Lina focuses, taking each turn with care.
"Watch me, Jules!" she shouts. Jules laughs and stays close behind her.
"Don't take too many risks!" he reminds her.
Lina feels free and fast, but she knows she must stay focused to drive well.

A PROBLEM TO OVERCOME

Suddenly, Jules encounters a little problem. His kart stops! Lina doesn't hesitate for a second. She slows down and stops next to him.
"What's wrong, Jules?" she asks.
"I don't know, it won't start!" he replies, a bit worried.
Lina smiles. "Don't panic, I'll help you!" She encourages him, and together, they manage to restart the kart.
"Thanks, Lina!" Jules says gratefully.

END OF THE RACE

The race is coming to an end. Lina crosses the finish line, her heart racing. Even though she didn't come in first, she feels proud. Jules arrives just behind her.
"Well done, Lina!" he exclaims. "Every race is a lesson, and I learned a lot today!"
Lina smiles and replies, "Yes, and I had so much fun!"

LESSON LEARNED

At the end of the race, Lina and Jules meet up with their friends. "What did you learn today?" one friend asks.
"That teamwork and safety are essential!" Lina says.
Jules adds, "And that the most important thing is to have fun together!"
All the kids nod, smiling. They are ready to keep learning!

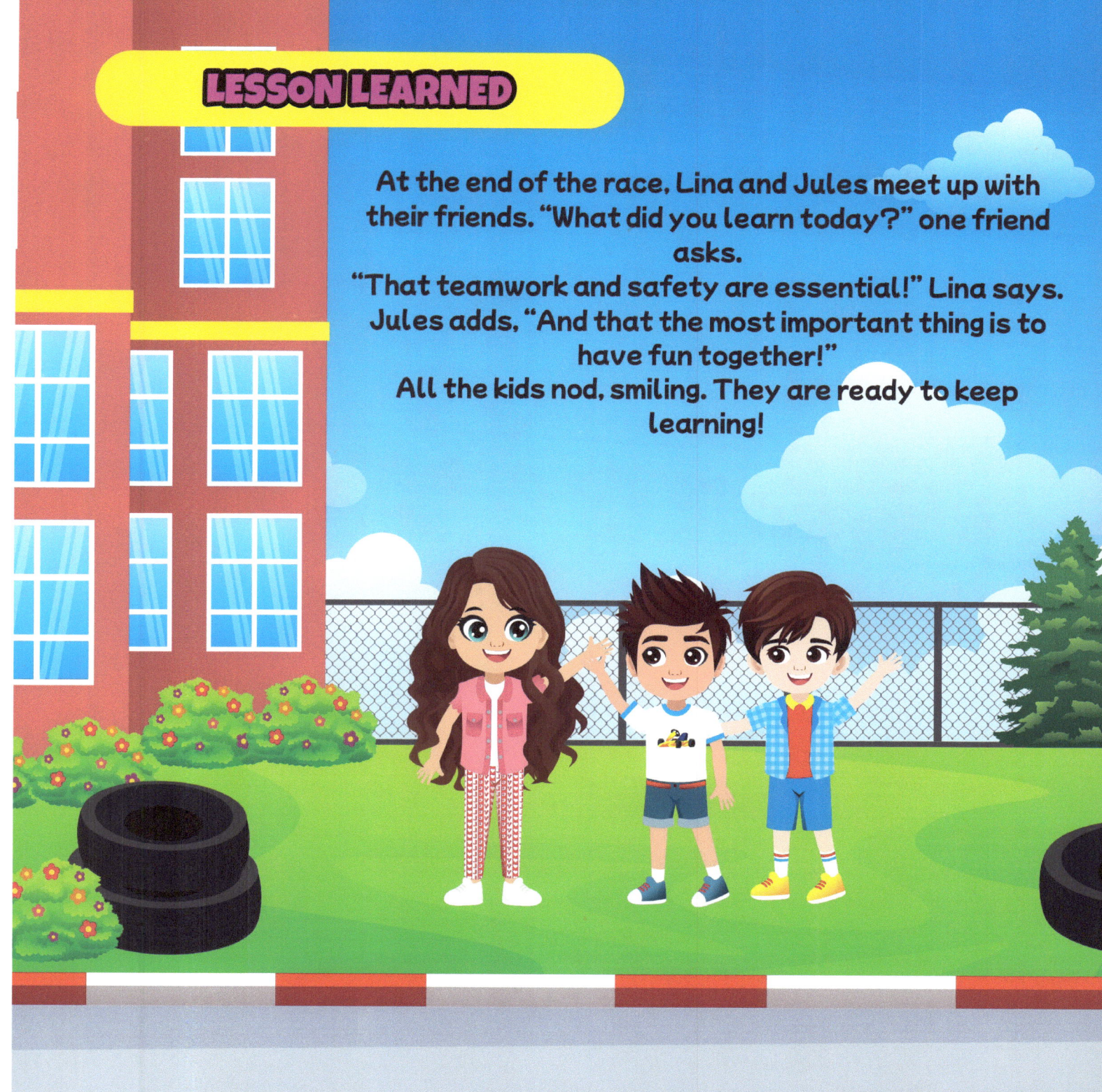

DREAMS AND AMBITIONS

Lina looks at the champions' board. "One day, I'd like to be up there!" she says, pointing at the drivers. Jules smiles at her. "You can do it, Lina! You just need to believe in yourself and keep practicing!" Lina feels encouraged. "Thank you, Jules. I'm going to keep training!"

NEXT ADVENTURES

Lina and Jules are both eager to return to the track. "Next time, I'm going to train even harder!" Lina declares. Jules nods in agreement. "Me too! And maybe some other friends will want to join us." Lina smiles. "Yes, the more the merrier!"

UNITY ACROSS THE WORLD

Lina and Jules discover photos of young drivers from around the world. "Look at these kids karting in Italy, Australia, and Japan!" says Jules. "Karting is a sport that brings everyone together!"

Lina nods in agreement. "YES! No matter where we come from, we all share the same passion!"

READY FOR THE FUTURE

Lina and Jules learned a lot today. They know that karting is more than just a race. It's a place where friendships are made, important values are learned, and big dreams can take flight. They are ready for their next adventures on the track!